Mike Watts is a writer/spoken word performer from Hull, England. His first collection *A Street Near You* was published in 2010.

Day and Night in the Damaged Goods Factory

Mike Watts

Burning Eye

Copyright © 2013 Mike Watts

The author asserts the moral right under the Copyright, Designs and Patents Act 1988 to be identified as the author of this work

All rights reserved. No part of this publication may be reproduced, stored in a retrieval system, or transmitted, in any form or by any means without the prior written consent of Burning Eye Books, nor be otherwise circulated in any form of binding or cover other than that in which it is published and without a similar condition being imposed on the subsequent purchaser.

This edition published by Burning Eye Books 2013

www.burningeye.co.uk

@burningeye

Burning Eye Books
15 West Hill, Portishead, BS20 6LG

ISBN 978 1 90913 617 5

Printed in Scotland by Bell & Bain, Glasgow

CONTENTS

Night Terror	7
Burlesque	8
Six Beers	9
Burn	11
Cheers	12
Arthritis and Debt	14
Corky	16
Edinburgh	17
Three More Days	19
Bring Me Sunshine	21
… And Some You Lose	22
'86 Orion	24
House Sitters	25
Still No Change	26
Going Quietly	27
Him and Me	29
Gunpowder	30
Limp	32
Medicine	33
My Turn at Sadie's	34
No Guarantee	35
By Nature	36
Not a Single Tulip	37
Scorching	39
Round 25	40
Like in the Movies	42
I Kid You Not	43
Bombshell	46
Crime Scene	47
Earwig	49
Detroit	51
As It Was	52
Comfort	53
Reunion	54
Bet My Day	56
Venus	57
Big Danny's Girl	58

1.30pm, 2nd Floor. Mr. Jacobs	60
This Happened	61
Deleted	63
Coming Up with the Goods	65
What Trees?	66
Goldie	67
The Referral	68
Mad	69
Sketches and Zeppelins	70
Iron	72
The Last of My Things	73
Repeat Performance	74
I, Thief	75
In and Out of Sweet Lady Luck	76
Once Again	77
Only The Good	80
Stuntman	82
Pops	84
Suspended	85
Reasons to be Cheerful	87
Thinking Back	90
Me and Her	92
In One Hand	96
Slave To It	93
Lifer	95
Circle Jerk	96
Being Bothered	98
I'm Back	99

NIGHT TERROR

The Toms around here carry on like
Drunken gangs, upsetting bin lids
And bottles, fighting over females
And fish heads,
I am shaken by their madness
As they weave, hissing and spraying
Amongst the shadows.

The moon brings out the worst in them:
When bulbs are cooling
And toilets suck away
A final piss,
I listen as they scream
Like burning witches.

Unsettled, I step into my slippers
And stand at the window.
There is nothing,
Only rows of unlit terraces
And alleyways and dull cars
And the throat-slashing sense
Of something shocking
About to happen,
As I crawl back into bed
And wait.

BURLESQUE

In black silk and lace,
Her thighs cream
And her face
Emulsioned
A delicate shade,
Making her lips
Bleed almost
As she drenches
The mic,
Purring her sex,
Prowling
Like a panther
Around tables of men
Lost in dreams
Of a heat
They'll never know.

So they raise
Their beers,
Imagine it
Through whoops
And cheers
As she bends
And splits
And all the bits
She's fed them
Are filed away,
Logged in every
Memory bank.
And tonight
When it's cold
And there's no-one
To hold,
At least half
Will thank her
For that.

SIX BEERS

April was a Bingo friend of my mother's,
Seventy years old with jet black hair
And a shock of gold teeth
Stacked across her gums like bullion.

I'd been offered fifty pounds to paint her shed
And as much as I despised
That sort of thing,
The money clinched it.

I fired up my silver Nissan
And drove across the city to her house.

I'd put on an old jacket
And brought with me the two tins of
Slate grey that she wanted.

I'd shelled out for them the previous day
And expected to see it back
On top of the fifty.

She lived in a modest bungalow
With leaded windows, circular lawn,
And an ornamental well,
Thick with weeds.

I rattled the letterbox and waited.

She appeared at the window and gestured I'd
Go round the back.

She was waiting at the gate,
Smoothing down the ears of a huge dog.

As I approached
It reared up like a Sasquatch,
Its thick pink tongue dangling from a mouth

I didn't trust.

After several reassurances
I shuffled past and began to crack on.

Stretching,
Crouching,
Up and down steps,
On my knees,
At it until my right arm,
Wrist and shoulder,
Were dead.

The morning crawled to early evening
And I was done.

April came out from the house
Clasping her hands,
Her smile flashing like a jeweller's tray.

She circled around
Thanking me again and again,
Before pulling out three tens and a twenty
From her purse.

After fuelling up the car
And putting back what I'd laid out
For the slate grey,
There was enough left for six beers,

Which just about finished the job.

BURN

She's moved in
And her panties are slouched across
Every radiator and in the kitchen
Fruit piles like windfalls and the whole
Place exhales a new freshness.

Having her here for more than just sex
Has taken some getting used to.

I mean,
There is only one toilet,
One bed side table,
One lamp.

She is leading me to new experiences –
Seeds and soya milk –
Books that explore my inner self.

Yes, she has moved in
And her panties are slouched across
Every radiator and in the kitchen
Fruit is rotting and the whole
Place doesn't feel like mine anymore.

Having her here just for sex
Worked for us both.

Now I queue to piss
And in the bedroom
We broke the lamp in a fight.

Today
I am dumping putrid mush onto
The compost,

Watching flies as they
Rise and fall,

Like my empire.

CHEERS!

My motor insurance was due out
And I was fifteen quid short.
It was a Tuesday Afternoon;
The bank was almost empty and I was
Attended to straight away.

The cashier was called Doreen.
She had big fat fingers
And huge drooping breasts
That seemed to disappear beneath
The counter.

I pushed two tens through
And watched as she pulled
Out the cash drawer.

When I saw all of the 50's and 20's,
I was reminded of Monopoly.
All that money,
I used to drool in the fantasy.

She slid me back a five
And asked if there was anything else
That she could help me with.
Not in a thousand years baby,
I said to myself.

I had three pound coins
In my pocket
So I crossed the road to the bookies.
The number ten had been on my mind
All day.

I slotted in a nugget,
Shut my eyes and stepped back.
Ten black,
Said the automated bitch

Inside the machine.

I clenched my right fist
And bared my teeth.

The previous day
I'd been at the funeral
Of a friend of the family
And someone had pointed out
How weird it was
That he'd died on the 10th of the 10th
And that the service kicked off
At 10am.

I cashed in the £36 slip
And made my way up the street
To the mini market.

When I got home,
I fell back into a chair
And yanked open a can of strong
Polish lager.

I took a long slug,
Wiped my lips and raised it
To good old Harry.

ARTHRITIS AND DEBT

Raking a nostril at my lap-top,
I see a spider crawl out
From between my old trainers.

Garlic to a vampire.

I roll a finger around my thumb,
Await its next move.

Sensing my fear,
It moves forward,
Scurries across the laminate
In a do or die charge.

I close the lid and withdraw.

Owned once again
By a fearsome inch
Of hideousness
I have no answer to,

I resettle in the kitchen
And start again.

I'm looking at a poem
That I rediscovered
Yesterday.
An unfinished,
Half-pissed scribble
With a good first line
That could save it.

I uncork a red
And go at it until there is
No sunshine,
My screen a square of light
In the cool dark

As I fall in and out,
Creating,
Deleting,
Still thinking of that spider,
Triumphant
In the other room.

Years ago,
I destroyed one
And took a back-hander
From my dad.

It's unlucky, he said.

He didn't lie.

CORKY

Lives down Saffron Terrace and hoards crap.

Split buckets, worn tyres, three legged chairs,
He'll stack his barrow and wheel it home.

Number 22 is a shit-hole.
Newspaper fades behind every window,
And the front gate, hanging by a hinge,
Has PERV sprayed across it.

A few weeks back, the police came
After an Ariel fitter claimed he'd seen him
Masturbating on his shed roof.

He owned a one-eyed dog that never stopped.

Last winter, it was found solid by the postman
After a big freeze, and Corky,
Pissed and wailing, torched it in the garden.

Toothless and skinny,
He wears ex council overalls
And his hair,
A shiny nicotine yellow,
Dangles in greasy curls from his shrunken head.

Yesterday, my mother spoke to a former resident
Of Saffron Terrace.

She said that she and her boyfriend had moved away
Because Corky would throw tea-bags at their washing

And he also played Kenny Rogers – full blast!

EDINBURGH

Step out of the Banshee Labyrinth
Through suds
Of freshly swilled sick
Up the cobbled slope
To the Mile
Where crowds slice through
Like cavalry and
Thousands of flyers
Are thrust like sabres
As we are swept along
In a tsunami of bodies
Past windows
Of whiskies and tartans
And performers
Of every kind
Feeding us tasters
To tempt us
As we are rocked
Back and forth
Dazzled
By the sheer stretch
Of it
And when the skies
Darken
And every bin is
Overflowing
With shiny squares
Of names and faces
They glide in –
Night gulls
The fast food angels
And little escapes
The zooming black
Of beady eyes
As we meander
Spitting and spilling
Crusts and fries

Still hoping to discover
Better shows
And cheaper beer
As they pick
Around us
Feathered phantoms
Of a rock-hard
City
That I'm taking on
Again
Next year.

THREE MORE DAYS

Alone for three weeks
In a bed that has
Crippled me,
Whose sheets have tormented
To the edge of
Insanity
And tonight,
As bleak northern bursts
Pelt rain at my
Window,
Wanting nothing more
Than to feel
The warm plump
Of breasts
Soft at my back.

I am here
And she is 250 miles south
Of hands
That would peel
Her like fruit
If she were beside me now.

Heavy as I am,
Sleep touches briefly
And the need
To piss
Is about to break it
Completely.

There is too much space.

I want
An entanglement of legs,
An arm locked
Around my chest,
I want to close my eyes

Until the point
Of an elbow
Digs a rib
And wakes me.

BRING ME SUNSHINE

It's bitter walking to the post office
And I've acknowledged at least a dozen faces
I'm acquainted with.

Despite the deep depression
I've never seen this street so rammed,

Even the queue for fish is ridiculous

And there are long lines at each cash point
Where again I have to nod and smile.

Smile.

Despite the wettest April on record
And a warning of more to come,

The post office is bustling
With mothers mostly
And a baby, screaming itself crimson
Fractures my thoughts.

I collect a passport form and leave.

Outside on the street
Something with dead haddock eyes
Holds out a hand for change.

I wave it away,
Pull my collar up over my ears,

As the first of that forecast drops like bombs.

... AND SOME YOU LOSE

Sent a text to the wrong one
And now I'm in the shit

You see I've been having my cake
And gorging on it

Sadly that's how it goes
When we drift off course

When we lap at pools
Different from those
That we are duty bound
To drink

The new flavours weaken us

We never think
For more than a second
Of consequence

We drown happily
In our filthy ignorance

And there are victims
World's will crumble
Be it 'full blown'
Or a fumble
In the back of a car
Someone's bound to see

And you'll be exposed
Believe me

I'm in limbo now
A wandering soul
I've got absolutely zilch
When I had it all

I played and gambled
Mindless of cost

Bet it all on number one
– And lost!

'86 ORION

Heading south in her MOT failure,
We spluttered through villages that blew no litter,
Where properties relaxed in landscaped acres,
Where 4x4's cooled on neat red brick,
Where the retired mowed and watered,
Where greenhouses glinted and horses munched.

And when our radiator spewed its last,
We stopped in a place called 'Swan Ellerker',

With its weather veins and pond,
With its monument and church,
With its dovecots and honey for sale.

A clotted cream scone of a village
That the rusting hulk we were in
Added to like dung,

And its little shop was whitewashed,
And the water expensive,
And the woman who served,
Sharp and cold,
And at those prices we shared a pie.

Because with a hundred to go,
And the situation being what it was,
I knew we'd have to stop again.
And these places being what they are,
We'd need every fucking penny.

HOUSE SITTERS

The door bell is relentless
As you clutch each ankle,
Gasp at the circling of my tongue
In the front room,
Curtains closed,
Feet away from whoever's there.

"Fuck 'em", I say.

Ride these two fingers,
Working like bony pistons,
My third and fourth
Pumping through the slush
Of your heat.

Cheap vodka's undressed us
And everyone's in Lanzarote
So let's finish this shit.

GOD!
Wish they'd fuck off.

WE'RE NOT IN!

STILL NO CHANGE

I have pillared together
A dish of copper and made 8 piles.
This equates to £4,
Or thereabouts.

Now I am going to humiliate myself
At the bank.

Yesterday I had £60
But I fancied a horse named
Magic Mike.

I threw a twenty at him
And then ten more,
On a dog whose name
Escapes me.

Two defeats had me 30 down.

Thirty became zero
And I assaulted myself
To the side of the head
All the way home.

Inside the building,
My shame is heavy
As I chew a nail and
Taste the counting
Of coin.

The cashiers are immaculate.

Jackie's my favourite,
A tanned brunette with
Whitewashed teeth.

I lie to her a lot.

I need a good one
Now!

GOING QUIETLY

The taste of things,
I'll miss when I'm dead;
The fry-up,
The fanny,
The freshly baked bread,

And smells,
I'll miss them too;

Tarmac as it's
Being rolled,
The drift of
Someone's barbecue,

And sight,
I'll miss seeing

The world and all
Its shapes and colours;
– My girlfriend peeing.

And touch;
Never to feel

The back of a head
As it bobs
Up and down,
The flesh inside
A dressing gown,
A cool breeze,
The trickle of sweat,
Whisky as it hits
The throat –
A cigarette.

And yet

As much as thunder
Excites me,
And the slap
Of doggy delights me,

The
Crying, lying,
Bullying, dying,
Bombing, bashing,
Screaming, smashing,
Threatening, plotting,
Snivelling, snotting,
Shooting, looting,
Skull-polluting,
That runs
Through my ears
Like piss.

I can tell you
Now for nothing,

I won't miss.

HIM AND ME

The luckiest man on earth
Is content with his life
With his nothing job,
His dull wife.

The luckiest man on earth
Has no ambition
No desire to win,
He has no passion.

The luckiest man on earth
Is free of debt
Sleeps well at night,
He doesn't bet.

The luckiest man on earth
Has burnt his books
Despises all art,
Thinks poetry sucks.

The luckiest man on earth
Couldn't give a shit
As I scream in the dark,
His opposite.

GUNPOWDER

Scissoring my toes as things
Whizzed
And banged
Outside
And the volume up
Almost full
So I could hear
The 30 something classy blonde
As she
Smiled and pointed at the
British Isles dotted
With little grey clouds and
Yes
I would
I thought to myself
As a small atom bomb split
The street outside
Making me jump
And somebody
Cheered as an alarm went off
And my recently widowed
Neighbour screamed FUCKING HELL
Through the thin
Walls and then more
Screams
As a succession of hisses
Cracked and
Exploded
And as I stood up
To brush the bits
From my dressing gown
Noticed my
Phone had three
Missed calls and a text
To say
Tried to call but no reply

Gone to my mums
Instead
See you Wednesday
X

LIMP

Yesterday morning on her way to work,
She clipped a cat near the railway bridge,
Snapping its back.

She rang me in floods of tears.

She said it was wearing a collar
With a small disc attached to it,
There was a phone number on one side
And the name 'Clive' on the other.

I jotted down the number and promised
That I'd ring straight away.

When I called a woman answered
And I broke the terrible news.

I felt so bad I offered to drive to the spot
And if the cat was still there,
Deliver its body over to her house.
It was still there.

The woman was waiting at the front gate,
Chewing a thumb nail.

I handed her the limp parcel.

She'd had him 17 years and he was almost blind.
She said her son would find a spot for him
In the garden when he returned home
From work.

That evening whilst being ridden in my chair
I thought of the days events and lost
My erection.

I apologised and she went to make a start
On the washing-up.
It had been an unusual day for us both.

MEDICINE

My neighbours battle constantly:
She slaps him with ugly pig,
And he uppercuts back with
Fat bitch.

Sometimes when they start
I turn off the radio,
So that I can tune in
To their violence.

I don't understand
How two people would want
To share the same space,
To eat and sleep together.

Tonight there is a truce:
I can hear laughter from their TV
So I switch on the radio
And re-read a letter from
My landlord.

He's finally sending someone
To sort out the damp in
My bathroom.

I've done it alone
For almost a year now,
There's been real pain
But I'm getting used to it —

Good friends and distraction
Such as this
Have saved me.

I can't imagine
Anything more terrible
Than being choked to death
By loneliness,
By silence.

MY TURN AT SADIE'S

Stretched out,
Jeans to my knees,
Watching her oily grip shaping me
Into something usable.

The TV on mute
The room stinking of beer and smoke.

Three kids in bed –
One at dad's,
A bulb with no shade,
Paper that's peeling,
Hamster at its wheel
And her thumb texting
Christ knows who
As I curl my toes,
Determined to get there
As she slaps away,
The one handed potter,

Who's never lost one yet.

NO GUARANTEE

She's an Auxiliary at the Infirmary and whenever she stays over,
She needs to be up and out for seven.

Her routine is simple: strip wash, moisturise, tie back hair,
Apply lippy, eat toast, refresh lippy.

I'm doing nothing at the moment but I like to get up with her,
Fill the kettle, pop a slice under and then nip out to unlock the gate;
The bolt's rusty and takes some effort to slide open.

When I know she's sorted I shuffle back to bed
And scramble about in a dream for an hour or so.

Downstairs, the scene is always the same:

A tea bag in the sink, crumbs in the bathroom,
A tap running, make-up on the mirror, a light left on,
Milk left out, little things that really grip my shit.

She tells me I'm anal.

She may have a point.

Other than that she's a real diamond, working long hours
Whilst I crash in and out of charity shops looking for lost Picassos
And signed Hemingway firsts.

All I'm saying is she's got her faults
And I've got mine,

We are what we are.

BY NATURE

The guy who runs the hardware store beats his partner.
It's common knowledge.
They live in the flat above and she works for him.
She's thin and quiet and her mysterious eyes
Never leave the floor –

But she knows where everything is:

Turpentine
Blue tack
Wire wool

She'll find and bag it without ever lifting her head.

She only ever speaks when she has to
And the horrible cardigans and long grey skirts
Are probably his choice.

Mrs Garvey's been using the store since it opened,
She said he bruised and bullied his former wife for years
Until she finally found the guts to leave.

I saw him yesterday afternoon lifting boxes of varnish
From out of the back:

A huge, sweaty mess with medicine ball head on a fat
Blubber neck.

The sign above his shop reads: DICK'S DIY.

Enough said.

NOT A SINGLE TULIP

After an iced coffee,
We crossed a couple of canal bridges,
And entered the Red Light area

Women and girls
Seated in glass boxes,
Sucking on cigarettes,
Legs yawning,

Little honeycombs of everything;

Hysterectomy scars,
Punctured tits,
The booze,
The boyfriends,
The beatings

And then the beautiful,
The fresh,
The star buys,

Doing it for college,
For cars,
For Christmas,

In every window,

All of them,

Distracted,
Unconvincing.

After purchasing some handcuffs
We headed off for
Breakfast,

A Traditional English with tea
Cost around €7.

Inside the Café de Jaren
We sat and deleted photos that
Neither of us
Were happy with,

Whilst our order
Sizzled
In the back somewhere.

SCORCHING

Cool – in my shorts and £5 shades,
I pedal to buy beer for my fridge.

It's late June: the sun is fuming,
And I am thrilled to burn beneath it.

To my left and to my right the beautiful
Distract me;

Summer is not a season for single men.

Outside the shop,
A tethered dog licks lazily at its balls.

I have no lock. I chance it,
Lean it up against a window, where headlines
Claim we are baking better than
Florida.

Inside, a girl with tattoos and bejewelled navel
Takes my twenty.

I hang a bag of six over my handlebars
And head back home.

The sky is a stretch of merciless blue,
And I think of these lagers and of breasts
And legs.

In two days July begins.
No respite.

ROUND 25

Apparently I took her without her consent
And I am an unholy bastard.
She gouged me, split my lip and smashed
My Beatles mug.

During the act she clawed my arse,
Pushed my head down onto her breasts,
And eventually came.

She's been married twice
And if her stories are genuine,
I'm the only one who hasn't chinned her.

Amongst other crap,
She's tried to poison me,
And invites herself into my wallet
Whenever I sleep.

On the night of the alleged molestation,
We were watching porn and drinking Vodka.
The girls were drenched and sexy.
She said I wanted them.
Of course I wanted them.

10 minutes into it, she hit the pause
And told me to lie alongside her –
I shuffled across and we began to play a little.

Soon I was working away,
And that's when she started:

"Ooh, you SHIT! Those DIRTY BITCHES,
Get off me, GET OFF ME!"

Her tongue snaking around mine,
Hips and buttocks grinding, eyes rolling,
Nails pinching and digging.

Look, I love the silly bitch to bits
But we argue all the time,
And believe me,
We've had this one many times.

LIKE IN THE MOVIES

If she were dead,
She wouldn't be able to taunt me
With her lovers.

But I'm no killer,

And I can't leave
Because
Even if I had a place to go,

I haven't the guts.

So I just pour the whisky,

Close my eyes,

And imagine that some tough
Handsome son-of-a-bitch

Was me.

I KID YOU NOT

All this happened the day after
I'd slugged
The ice-cream man.

I'd nipped out to buy
A light bulb.

I was fifty yards down the street
When this pissed off
Bull Terrier
Came steaming toward me.

I was rooted.

It smashed into me and began
Tearing at my thigh.

It was agony as its huge
Muscle head shook and slavered.
Then, after ten lifetimes,
The bastard unclamped me
And trotted off.

A little Asian guy,
Shaking behind a bike,
Helped me to my feet.

I fell back against a wall,
Torn denim flapping
Around my knee.

A crowd gathered and an
Ambulance arrived
Within minutes.

After a clean up and stitches,
I was left behind curtains,

Bandaged and naked
From the waist down.

A young nurse poked her
Head through.
I cupped my cock and balls
As she pushed a needle
Into my arm
And said I was free to go.

I limped into a taxi at
Around seven o'clock.
It had just started to drizzle.

The driver had very little to say
And that was fine,
I just needed to get home.

We stopped at lights.

It was a quiet, uneventful journey –

Until his door was ripped open
And he was punched and
Slapped and wrestled around
The car.

I froze again
As a hooded lunatic savaged him,
Before making off with
His cash bag.

The police dropped me off
At about half nine.

I stepped into my kitchen and flicked
The switch: Shit!

No bulb.

In the fridge there were two cans.
I let the first hit of cold lager
Settle around my tongue.

My life and my Levi's were fucked!

And there was still that other crap,
The ice-cream man,

Now there's a story...

BOMBSHELL

When I walked in after Petra it was atrocious;
It was like bouncing off a brick wall; my face
Hit the back of my head, my nose writhed and twisted,
My eyes streamed as if poked and peppered,
And she just brushed past me, smiling,
Buttoning-up her jeans as if we'd been together
Twenty years. That such a petite, intelligent, unassuming
Little doll could be responsible for that.

We'd spent most of the evening on the couch
Experimenting with sexual positions.
She was light and supple and very creative
And by 11 o'clock we'd added another page to the
Karma Sutra. I made us hot milk, pulled out some plugs
And then we went straight to bed.

I awoke at 8:15 went downstairs, made us both a tea,
Picked out a few biscuits, brought it all back up on a tray
And then climbed back in beside her.
We finished it, had a cuddle, gave each other
Oral sex, got dressed and then came down.

She was 15 years my junior, training to be a chemist,
Half-Portuguese and this was our first night together.
I'd spent all day vacuuming and bleaching and polishing,
I put on clean sheets and pillow cases, I took two showers,
I even bought scented candles.

Look, sometimes we stink; it happens, that's not the problem,
The problem is, there was Summer Fresh and a window in there
And she didn't use either of them. Maybe I'm over-reacting,
But this morning a line was crossed, we've only
Known each other a few days and as taut and trim
And as accommodating as she might be,

I just know, despite the fact we probably had a few more
Pages to write, I'll never be able to look at her
In the same way again.

CRIME SCENE

I'm sinking
My cold bare flesh
Into the hot shock
Of clear steaming water
And as I hit the enamel,
A sudden burst of yellow
Mushrooms out
From between my legs:

The relief's incredible,
Intense,
Like a surprise death-row pardon,
And as it encircles me,
I have a thought –
I reckon
That I've been shit on
Just about everyday
Of my entire working life.

But it's Saturday morning
And it's no big deal
And I'm content to be sitting here
Lassoed,
By my own piss,
In my own bath.

Except today
It's not my own bath,
Today there are two lots of towels,
A pink razor,
And different shampoos
And today
I'm at the tap-end,

And she's unclipping her bra
And I'm using the back of my hand
As a paddle

Distracting her,
With talk of shopping
Before she kicks off her knickers
And joins me,
In the soothing heat
Of a terrible secret.

EARWIG

I was queuing at the post office,
Listening to a fat man
Who owned his own garage,
Spouting to the cashier how he just loved
All of the snow and ice,
Because he was earning a fortune,
And he hoped it would continue
For at least another six months,
Because he wanted to buy the spare land
At the back of his house
And build flats on it.

His white Walrus belly hung over his jeans
From inside his long leather coat,
And I hated him.

I imagined losing control of something heavy,
Crushing him up against a wall and
Spilling his thick flabby tripe
Everywhere.

When it was my turn to be served,
I whispered that the guy was an arsehole,
And the cashier nodded.

We did the business
And then I made my way to the little shop part
To buy mints.

A pregnant woman walked in and began stamping
Her boots on the tiles.

I heard her mention to a girl tidying envelopes
That at least another inch had fallen
And that the forecast was shocking.

Outside I saw the fat guy

Inside a big black 4x4 with a mobile phone
Pressed to his ear
He looked up through the screen,
Then threw his head back laughing.

I zipped up my jacket,
Popped an extra strong into my mouth
And headed off toward 'Garrett' the butcher.

It was a ten minute walk
But his steak and gravy pies were legendary
And I just hoped,
As my ears began to freeze,
I wouldn't have to queue there.

DETROIT

Half-pissed in the kitchen,
Waiting for drying,
The drum rattling,
Exhaling
Hot gasps
As I wipe a
Thumb print
From my glasses
And notice
She's left 2 down;
The motor city
7 letters
Ends in t.

I unscrew a new bottle
And neck a
Mouthful
As I fold
Neatly
My black denim.
She's out until ten
And I'm
Drinking again
But if I remember,
I'll text her,
Later,
The answer.

AS IT WAS

The shower light's been left on

The cheap coffee's gone

I've been asked where I've been

I can smell Mr Sheen

There's a liner in the bin

My pornography's missing

There are clean sheets on the bed

The plants have been fed

My balls feel much lighter

The future looks brighter

And all in one day

What can I say?

…She's back!

COMFORT

The problem we have is we scrap
About nothing,
Then one of us walks out.

Yesterday it was my turn.

I unchained my bike
And made for the bridge,

It worked for me there.

That ancient hunchback
Of local stone,
Scarred and sturdy,
And beneath it,
Clear shallows,
Idling at no great pace,
But enough to pacify,
Even as I make a fist and smash it
Into my palm,
Curse through my teeth,
Gob out whatever it is that's blistering
Inside.

After a good hour,
I threw my last rock
And pedalled back.

We blanked each other in the yard,
The fresh smell of citrus flapping
About us,
Her blonde hair lifting
And re-settling,
Teeth clamped around a towel,
As she pegged out washing.

REUNION

Relaxing
With the radio
Letting beer
Do its business
Before drifting
Into the strangest
Dream

A balloon-trip
Over the estate
Where I grew up

Floating
In a basket
With the dead
Of my past

A grandmother
Two aunties
Pets and school friends
Killed by cars
By suicides
A favourite teacher
My first two-wheeler

These ghosts
These things
Flying with me
Over the high rise
(Demolished now)

And my school
(Razed by
Match strikers
Too young
To punish)

All of us

Embracing
Crying
Big tears of
Remembrance

Coming round
I adjusted
The volume
And stretched out
For another bottle

Time chips away
At everything
Shrinking our world
With its hunger
For
Rot and rust

Right now
I'm thinking about
Yesterday
And that beer driven
Twenty minutes

Where I got to see
Them all again

BET MY DAY

Taking a short cut across the lorry park,
I passed three gulls picking at the headless stink of a big fish.
As I got nearer, one became uneasy and fucked off.
The other two braved me for a few more seconds,
Then screeched away.

I was on my way to settle a debt.

I owed Marcus ninety pounds. He was a good mate
And it wasn't the first time he'd bailed me out,
I was a gambler.

I'd just turned into Brentwood Terrace
When I crashed into his on-off partner, Janice.
She was hysterical; "GET AN AMBULANCE!"

Marcus didn't look right and she'd left her phone.
I did as she asked and then followed her back into
The house.

She led me upstairs into the front bedroom.

As soon as I stepped inside, I could smell him;
His fat, aubergine face bursting out from under a blue quilt.

They'd rowed about his drinking a few days ago
And she'd gone back to her dad's.

Two emergency vehicles pulled up outside
And I was questioned for over an hour.

I needed a shot of something.

The Swan Inn was just around the corner,
Wedged between Mina's Deli and a William Hill.
I pushed open a door and pulled out a roll of notes.
Perfect, I thought, I can have a drink anytime.

VENUS

Only one side of the curtain is closed as the moon
Torches light into the room.

A tantalising fancy about money has rocked me awake
And I'm fingering my nose, pondering.

I'm on my arse and these dreams are torturous.
I owe a little something to almost everyone
And I need to dig deep to resolve it.

My everyday is pretty much the same but having a
Sexual partner sugars it slightly.

She's laying beside me now, her plump lips well parted.
I tweezer a finger and thumb and remove thin strands
Of hair that she's sucked into a corner of her mouth.

She snakes out a tongue and makes a fist before re-settling.

I imagine the stuff that I pumped into her a few hours
Previously is still moving.

The crumpled shadow of knickers and a hairdryer
Begin to make sense as my eyes slowly un-glue.

I pull back the sheet –

Breasts, big and beautifully sculpted dominate the landscape
Of pale flesh as I circle a nipple with my thumb
And watch her sleeping.

BIG DANNY'S GIRL

Wakened by nausea
I make the sink
And let it go.

Too much of everything
Spreads itself,

A Jackson Pollock
Of booze and buffet
Hits the porcelain
As I heave and growl.

Emptied
I run the tap,
The back of my hand
Scraping across my
Chin.

I tug at a curtain.

Its late morning and
Daylight is a
Hot corkscrew
I'm not ready for,

I need to
Rehydrate,
To think straight.

Three fingers pushed
Against my brow
I trawl through
The bits in-between:

What did I do?
Where have I been?

To the right of me
There is money,
Some coins and a twenty,
And on the microwave
A torn strip of
Paper with a name
And number:

Shit!
I remember,
The red-head:

Carl
Answer your phone
Answer your phone
Carl,

That bird last night,

I'm dead.

1.30PM, 2ND FLOOR, MR. JACOBS

I have sparked up the gas,
Oiled the pan,
Dug a knife between two frozen discs
To split them,

And I don't think of
Saturates,
Or heart disease,
Only the sharp pangs building
In my gut.

Sometimes,
After the friend and his bottle
Have finally left,
And the only concern
Is the quickest way to cook
Those last few burgers,
It's easy to forget,
To stand there grinning
Like an imbecile,
Blank to the fact (as you flip them over),

If you miss this one…

THIS HAPPENED

After three beers and double rum
On a dead Sunday afternoon
I went home to bed and had a dream
That I lifted some flowers
From outside a shop
And then boarded a bus
To the cemetery
Where I dropped a single bloom
At the base of each
Neglected stone before
Stealing a bike
Belonging to an old man
Breaking his heart
Beside a freshly dug hole
And as I pedalled away
I too began to cry
Because it was just so sad
And as I sped out through
The cemetery gates
My grandad (who I'd never met)
Was standing there
Pointing a finger and shaking his head
But I just kept on pedalling
Faster and faster
Until sparks and flames
Began to erupt behind me
And then without warning
A small boy in a red shirt and bow tie
Stepped out from behind
An old blue Escort
And the small boy was me
And as I pulled back on the brakes
I was sent rocketing over
The handlebars
My arms pinned to my sides
Tearing like a missile through
A great expanse of white

And then
My eyes suddenly sprang open
And I felt a need to piss
So I got up
And made my way to the toilet
Where I unzipped the best
Hard on
I'd had for some time.

DELETED

The past is buried now,
200 feet down,
Quick-limed and
Concreted over,
Finished.
And every photographic
Reminder,
Scissored,
Bagged and dumped
Along with the
Valentines,
The birthdays
And all the other etc's.

I feel unusual sitting here
Typing this,
Hearing the fire's
Gentle hiss and
Looking out to see
A thin March snow
Pasted across
The roofs of cars
And houses.
For two years
My head's been kicked
Around,
Bounced against
Walls,
Thrown up in
The air and slugged
From one end
Of town to another.

It's been a long time coming,
But today,
It's as though torture
Has finally

Forgiven me,
She's sorted now
And I'm almost there.
This will be the
Last time I speak
Of it.

And as the 10am clouds
Begin to fracture,
I can hear next door
Singing as she
Vacuums,

Christ, I'm smiling,
It's over.

COMING UP WITH THE GOODS

I read other writers and it does nothing.
I walk amongst the dead and it does nothing.
I sit in darkened rooms and it does nothing.

I exchange insults with my partner,
Allow a cheap red to dance
Through my blood

And it never fails.

WHAT TREES? (After 'The Trees' by Philip Larkin)

The trees are coming into grief
You often hear it being said;
For new development, cut and dead,
It's ignorance beyond belief.

Is it that they'll grow again
As we grow old? No, it's not true.
They'll be replaced by something new,
Their loss is just another's gain.

Yet still the un-resting builders chop
For total profit everyday.
That's another green belt gone, they say,
Let's build a shop, a shop, a shop.

GOLDIE

Shaking it at the window
In her pink panties,
Raking through her thick auburn
Stretching and twisting,
A cock-straightening routine
Just for me –
Drunk at 10am,
With itchy five day growth
And the orange of his
Hospitalised neighbour's fish,
Floating freshly dead.

A good two minutes pass.

Slipping my hand down,
I push it to one side and turn away.

Too much of a good thing
Is still a good thing,
But all of this has got to stop.

And it will do.

Eventually.

THE REFERRAL

I step into a top floor room
With no windows.
Nick stands up to greet me;
30's, smooth-faced,
His hair blonde and spiky,
His teeth too good.

We sit down and I begin to speak.
He leans back,
Studies the ceiling.
Nods, smiles,
Chews his pencil
As I tell him of my fog,
Of the concrete that has replaced
My brain.

He begins drumming his palm,
To cross and un-cross his legs.

His diamond stud,
His pointed boots,
His framed certificates –
What on God's filthy earth
Am I doing here?

My 50 minutes end.
We'll continue this, he says.
Like fuck we will, I think.

And you see, that's my problem,
I can never say or do
What I'm really feeling,
Which is why I'm here,
Today.

MAD

Someone was slaughtered around here last night.
On the pavement, just outside the bike shop.
Dark patches are all that remain
Of an unnamed man in his forties.

Police are hoping that the words
         BASH OF N.H.E
Tattooed across the back of his neck
Will help to identify him.

I pick up the phone and finger the 9's.

Fuck me,
I was with him when he had that done.

How mad's that?

SKETCHES AND ZEPPELINS

To save on juice
I'm walking the three miles
Into town.

My books are going back
A week early,
And for me,
This is miraculous.

Tanya and Marie
Are just passing
As I drop the latch.

We all flash our teeth.

They share a house down
One of the terraces
And are known
Prostitutes.

The police visit
As often as anybody.

Four legs,
Two arses,
And a whole chunk
Of trouble,

I stay well clear.

Under my arm
There are
Autobiographies,
Edible fungi,
Roman glass,
And the latest
Record collector's price
Guide.

A heavy lot,
Doubled-bagged
With Tescos.

The library's good detox
For me.

Christine in local history
Is an old school friend.

A few years ago
She was awarded a CBE
For her championing
Of the disabled.

I wiggled a couple
Inside of her once,
When we were fourteen.

Whenever we catch eyes,
She pretends she
Doesn't know me.

I don't push it.

On the third floor
There's an inexpensive cafe
Doing good coffee.

And that's where I'm going.

Soon as I've found
Sketching for beginners,
And anything
On Zeppelins.

IRON

I've done three sets
Of barbell,
Dumbbell,
Standing press,
Shrugs,
And now,
Feeling the strain,
The ache,
And the downward drag
Of it all,
I'm resting.
Biceps ablaze with hot blood,
Staring
Into the big mirror,
Gulping bottled water,
Wishing myself
Far away from the
Grunt of this place,
Where it's only 8:30
And I'm watching meat-heads
Pushing twice my weight,
To beats boom booming
From a CD player,
Whilst outside,
Dangerous
Schoolgirls
Swear and smoke
Until the right
Bus comes.

THE LAST OF MY THINGS

This time last year, things were easy;
I awoke, I did, and then I slept.
It was uneventful, but it was painless.

Today, I'm talking to a small dog
Recovering from a mauling
That left her ripped and almost dead.
She's wearing one of those plastic cones
To stop her pulling at her stitches
And despite her misery,
I know she's listening.

The fur around her side has been shaved,
And as she rolls onto her back,
I can see that she is healing nicely.

My books are bagged
And I've left a note that speaks of apology,
And love.

Taking an apple from the bowl,
I leave my key
And walk away.

REPEAT PERFORMANCE

I dropped them to my knees,
Sat down,
And waited.

But there was nothing;
Nothing but the squeak and puff
Of feeble farts.

I was convinced
There would be something more
Solid.

I wiped anyway,
Pulled them up
And then went out
To fuel my car.

Tonight I was invited to a reading
At the university bar

I ordered a beer,
Sat down,
And waited,

But there was nothing.
Nothing but the squeak and puff
Of feeble farts

Which was exactly what I expected.

I, THIEF

It's born out of being
Skint;
Of being depressed
And crushed
By decisions
That I've made.

It's a disease of
Desperation,
Of simple
Madness.
It's an act of me
That I knew
Nothing of.

Now I am
Chameleon-eyed
And shifty,
Innocent until
Collared,
Guilty as sin.

Every other day
I buy one
And take one
Free,
Shameless as a
Squatting dog.

Me,
The black and white
Bandit,
Having it away
On CCTV.

IN AND OUT OF SWEET LADY LUCK

I was spooning rice pudding straight from the tin,
Listening to a debate on the radio about
Extortionate fuel costs.

I didn't own a car, so I didn't give a shit
But I could sense intense anger developing
And I was waiting for someone to lose it,
Perhaps pull a blade and open up a throat, live on air,

But instead it became an ear-ache
Of constant interruption and eventually,
I poked it off.

It was an overcast and miserable Friday, but
I was well on top.

I'd had an impressive run, two of my selections
Had romped in and the three home draws
I'd predicted paid me out a wedge,
So I was relaxed and contemplating
My next move.

It was always the same when I was in front.
When I wasn't chasing, I became bored.
The money was great, but it sedated me,
Lobotomised my urge to challenge whatever
It was I was up against;

When you hit cold concrete, you climb,

But I was fine, flabby with luck and with a roll of it
In my jeans pocket,
I knew exactly where I was heading.

I laced my boots and swaggered off back to the nearest,
Knowing full well she would fleece me,
Suck away the fat, flatten my heart into a burger,
And put some much needed steel
Back in my balls.

ONCE AGAIN

I'd had a few
But I jumped in and fired her up anyway.

I was on my way to see Byron.

Big Byron (a huge fat fuck of a fish merchant
Who dabbled in jewellery)
Could get his sausage fingers on anything
And I needed a gift to sweeten
A woman I'd let down.

I wasn't pissed by any means,
But at that time of the morning,
Easy game for any bored shitless two-man team
With time to kill.

I wound down the window for some air.

I got to thinking about Melissa.
She was a bit older than me and much wiser;
She'd travelled, was well-read and spoke
Good French.

I was supposed to have picked her up
Outside the University library at one o'clock,
But I was shooting pool
And necking cheap bitter in the 'Griffin'
With a couple of jobless buddies and it had
Slipped my mind –

Her message was simply – Prick!

She'd ignored my calls and texts all day
And I wanted to make it up to her.

Byron was selling gold St Christopher's
At a good price and though it was going

To cripple me,
I was desperate to get her one.

I was still ten minutes away,
The night air had turned into icy backhanders,
So I reversed the window
And began fiddling with the radio.

I was just turning left onto a mini-roundabout
When something shot out in front of me –

I felt an impact,
I slammed on and un-clipped my belt.
Stepping out onto the road,
I saw it,

A Fox!

I'd hit a Fox!

I stood over it, a beautiful thing
All sleek and gingery,
Its eyes staring, its chest heaving.

What the fuck was it doing here?
The cities were dangerous,
People were dangerous.

I climbed back into my car and began to think:

I can't just drive off, I can't leave it.

FUCK!

I was wary of being bitten,
But it was stiff with shock so I lifted it gently
And placed it onto the back seat.

There was an RSPCA centre
Fifteen minutes away,
I'll leave it there, somebody will discover it,
Save it,
It'll be running around again in a few days,
Stalking rabbits, tearing chickens heads off,
Being shot at,
Poisoned,
Persecuted.

I didn't sleep well.

I could have, I should have
Done more –

But that's me; I spread myself too thinly,
Nothing ever gets my full attention,
Sometimes I fall way too short,

I think we all do.

ONLY THE GOOD

And now that another has dropped
Well before his time,
I'm withdrawing what little money
I have left and pissing
Every penny of it up the wall
In memory of a good soul,
Lying cold as chrome
In storage somewhere,
And I shall argue
And slaver in memory of him,
And of our estate,
Where rolled up sleeves would
Always settle it,
Where beautiful mothers
Pegged out sheets,
Stuck on plasters,
And every day made
Something out of nothing.
Where we learned
To fight back,
To dream,
To shrug our shoulders
And carry on
Because we were as good
As anybody,
Despite the labels,
Despite the sneers.

If they say you can't,
Don't say you can,
Show 'em you can.
They're not better than
You son,
You're just as good
As they are.

Of course we were:

Our dads told us,
Beaten and bitter
In their failure,
We had to win –
For them.

Tonight I shall
Swing and miss,
Bleed from the nose,
Take on the world
In memory of him,

A good soul
Warm as toast,
In my heart.

STUNTMAN

The first time she came round to mine
She threw herself on the sofa and said,
"Go on then, do the honours."

It was black, no sugar.

She had a tattoo of a rose on her wrist
And a gap between her
Front teeth wide enough to hold
A cigarette.

I was crazy about her.

The last time I saw her,
I'd just finished showering.
I heard her come in
So I shuffled naked from the bathroom
Into the kitchen,
Drying my face with a towel.
I hadn't a clue what might happen,
Maybe I was hoping that
She might just push her tongue down
My throat and do me
Right there.

When she cried out
I pulled away the towel and feigned
Surprise before reversing
Back out of the room.
Seconds later the gate slammed
And a car fired up.

I remember pink jeans
And a pearl necklace.

If I'm totally honest,
It's not the first time I've

Done something like this.
A few years previously
It won me a slurping from my
Neighbour's sister.

I'm a terrible cunt, I know.

I rang to apologise and she said
Not to worry, but that was weeks
Ago.

I suppose that's that.

POPS

When she came home I took her bag
And just held her.
Not a single word passed between us.

We're both in our 40's
And she really didn't need this.

Imagine:
A spurt of love,
Sneaking through and ripping your guts out.

And then the guilt,
Having to sleep with it, wake to it,
And having nothing to fight back with
Except the promise
To always be there for one another.

You can never be certain of anything,
She swore that she never missed a day
And I believe that.

Well,
Time is running out for me,
For my ballerina, for my little bruiser,

I'm only sorry
We'll never kick a ball
Or fly a kite on a beach somewhere.

And though her daughter from a previous
Calling me Pops
Is nice,

It's just not the same.

SUSPENDED

I dabbed on Kouros, necked 4 pints,
Ogled some arse, played pool
And then went home to cold meat pie
And bed.

I dreamt I could run through walls,
Could smash through them like an exocet.
I'd hit them full on,
At supersonic speed, exploding rubble
And clouds of thick red dust
Upwards and everywhere.
I was unstoppable,
Invincible.

When I awoke,
I put on clean socks and came downstairs.

The postman had been.
I recognised the envelope,
White with a green band around
The middle.

I opened it,
Read it, shredded and binned it.

I unlocked the door
And hit the street,
Lunatic style –

Racing barefoot past pram-pushing,
Cig-sucking mothers,
Past dog walkers swinging
Little black bags,
My eyes streaming,
Feet and lungs burning,
Slicing through the air like a demented
Flesh bomb –

50 yards to go
And I'm eating-up concrete
Like an urban Leopard.
40.
30.
20: It's not the postman's fault –
Good, bad or indifferent,
It's his job.
10.
5.
4: The playing of ball games
    Is strictly prohibited.
3.
2: "YOU FUCKING WANKERS!"

Last night,
I dreamt I could run through walls
And believe you me,
I almost did.

REASONS TO BE CHEERFUL

December 2010
Was when it all
Went wrong,
When fortune turned
And landed one
In my face.

You see,
My life was cracking,
Then it broke,

After seeing my ex
With another bloke,
Which really hurt,
Because

The rotten
Bitch never wore
A short skirt
For me,

And since then,
Not a month's
Gone by
Without a kick in the
Bollocks,
Or a smack in the eye,

And this morning,
Just for me,
Just to perpetuate the
Misery –
My fucking freezer
Doesn't freeze,
I've got a car
But no car keys.
I'm being

Raped and mugged
By days like
These
And if it wasn't
So funny,
I'd have cried
When a Samaritan
Friend of a
Friend of mine
Suggested
That I suicide.

That's it.
It's time
To make plans.

So me,
My whisky,
My cannabis
And cans
Are having a party.

It's to celebrate
My new charity –

'Booze and Dope',
Raising hope
For the
Terminally unlucky,

And before you
Even think
Of racing round
To mine,
With your tears,
Your
Depression

And your cheap
White wine,
I wouldn't
Get too excited –

To be honest
It's just an
Excuse to get
Stoned and
Pissed

And I'm the
Only one
Invited.

THINKING BACK

A screech,
A bang,
A sensation of
Being pinned under
Heavy ice.

I remember
Slamming doors,
Frantic footwear,
And across my tongue,
A rich
Iron taste.

Then crowds of faces,
Mobile phones,
Strange mouths chewing
And bending.

'You'll be alright, mate.'

'He just stepped out.'

I recall
Spiralling upwards
Through
A thin mist,
Past my old school,
Past boxes
Of Pomegranates,
Past my grandmother
Rolling pastry.

That's what
I remember
Before a hot grinding
In my ears
Switched everything
Off.

ME AND HER

We were two drunks together,
And we were terrible –
Like a dog gone mental.

And when it kicked off,
We were like a thousand wasps
In a swarm of fury,
Like a hot and hungry
Pissed-off jury.

And then we'd just fall asleep,
Wake up to the TV blaring,
Sick and struggling –

Like a depressed mother,
A junkie brother,

Like a rejected suicidal lover.

But come payday
Came a well stocked fridge.
So when it was good
It was average.

But mostly it was bad.

And by Friday,
Behind the blue-grey cloud
Of our dwindling tobacco,
We would shake and cry,
Demand that each fuck off and die.

Which is what alcoholic lovers do
When the booze runs dry.

IN ONE HAND

I'd just dumped some broken panes of glass
In a neighbours skip, when two young lads
Came strutting toward me.
As they passed,
One of them snatched the cap off my head
And threw it into the road.

They didn't run,
They just carried on bouncing and talking
As if fuck all had happened.

When the police came I said
The reason I'd reacted the way I did was because
I was sick and tired
Of horrible little cunts like them,
Getting away with murder.

In the back of the car,
All I could think of was a cheque
That I was expecting from my publisher was due
To arrive and that Lizzy,
A bitch for attacking the mail,
Would destroy it.

I then began to wonder if I might
Get a custodial.
But one of the officers reckoned
Because of no previous
The worse case scenario would be a fine.

My first anthology had just hit the streets
And I'd managed to shift a few.
I was owed about two hundred pounds,
Hopefully that would cover it.

SLAVE TO IT

Anything can spark
The juice
And get it flowing.
I'll play the keys
Till my fingers bleed,
Delete it all
And start again.

Sometimes I'll balk
At the thought
Of rhyme,
I'd sooner slice
My genitals off,
I think it's all
A waste of time.

Quite often
My partner will swear
She loves it,
Then In a fit
Of vodka,
She'll rip it up
And say its shit.

Now there is venom
Flowing through
My blood,
I raise daggers over
Everyone,
Especially if they're
Good!

And I've strutted
And I've ranted
Like a fool on the stage,
With this demented
Idea,

It might pay me
A wage!

But the truth is,
I'm hooked
And it's a filthy habit,
Just sweating on my
Next line,
Like a slave
To it.

LIFER

I own a budgie called Spud.
I've had him four years.

His previous owner rotted
In the bath.

Two or three times a day
I push my face up against the bars
And talk at him.

He's never spoken back to me.

He escaped his cage once
And became entangled in the curtains.

Satan, my cat,
Is desperate to kill him.

Last night whilst shelling eggs,
I watched him butting his mirror
And wondered if he might be
Depressed.

If I was him, I would be.

CIRCLE JERK

I've read most of the
Great poets,
From such and such to
So and so.
Some have left me
Burning with admiration,
Inspired me
When I've been
At my lowest,
And I'm grateful to them
For that.

Today there are lots
Of people
Who call themselves
Poets.
It's a grand title,
And many are happy
To claim it,
But there are no
Great ones,
There haven't been
For a long time,
And now,
I feel as though
Poetry has stalled,
Pulled its own plug.
A bellowing
Has been replaced
By a whimper
As this growing band
Struggle for fire,
Or lap and tug
At one another
Until all are stroked
And sated.

Somewhere there is
A genius,
A he or she who is
Struggling to survive
The grind of
Minimum wage,
Vandalism,
Depression.
A writer
Throwing down
Thoughts in a way
That just might
Reignite and
Fill its veins
Again,

But don't hold
Your breath.

BEING BOTHERED

And here I am,
As always,
At the window,
Watching nothing unfold,
Lost in the fantasy
Of elsewhere,
As things are moved
By sudden breezes
And passing faces,
Grim as mine
Ponder whatever.

Slowly I return
And see that birds,
Fat on summer fruits,
Have scored directly,
And seed-filled purple
Has baked on hard.

To sort it,
I move outside,
Push into a shed
Twenty years rammed.

Spiders reverse
As new light gushes in
And dust hangs
In thin beams
As I shift and pull
At everything around me.

Bucket and sponge,
I remember you;
Show yourselves now,
Before the mood
Changes.

I'M BACK

It takes at least
An hour
For the small fire
To heat this room.

I stare hard
Into the flames.

All twenty digits
Ache with winter
And my ears
Are slapped.

There is little
Comfort here.

Above the fireplace,
I count
Nineteen cards.

Polar Bears
And Fat Santas
With their
Ho ho ho's.

Two days away
And I'm here again;

Cupboards empty,
Milk
Out of date.

Three years ago,
This house
Had a pulse,
A heartbeat:

Sex on the sofa,
A kitchen
Hot with cooking.

But none of that
Matters,
Because
The room is
Warming,
Blood is
Getting through
And there is
Feeling.

A feeling
Of ice melting,
A thaw,
Spring
Flowers,
Huge clear
Skies.

Some time ago,
During a
Period
Of madness,
I weighted my
Life with
Concrete
And threw it
Into the sea.

This is what
The tide
Washed up,

New flesh
On old bones,

A different
Person,
Me.

Acknowledgments:

Big thanks to Joe Hakim, Cilla Wykes,
My family and all those who have hung in there.
To Clive Birnie, for taking a punt.
And Russ Litten – cheers!